Thailand

Food and Agricultural Import Regulations and Standards

Section I. Food Laws:

The laws and regulations governing the Thai food industry are confined to the scope of the Food Act of B.E. 2522 (1979). The Act authorizes the Ministry of Public Health's Food and Drug Administration (FDA) to implement and administer the Food Act.

Under the Act, all establishments producing food for sale or importing food for sale must be licensed by the Food Bureau of the FDA. The application and granting of licenses must be in accordance with the principles, procedures or conditions prescribed in the Ministerial regulations, which are periodically elaborated, modified, and issued by the FDA's Food Bureau.

1.1 Food Act of B.E. 2522 (1979)

The Food Act of B.E. 2522 (1979) remains in effect. The Act defines the word "food" as edible items and those which sustain life including:

(A) Substances that can be eaten, drunk, dissolved in the mouth or induced into the body by mouth, no matter in what form, but not including medicine, psychotropic and narcotic substances.
(B) Substances intended for use or to be used as ingredients in the production of food including food additives, coloring, and flavoring materials.

The Act classifies food into four categories as listed below:

1. Specifically-controlled foods: Under this category registration is required. Legal provisions are established regarding standard quality, specifications, packaging and labeling requirements, as well as other aspects of good manufacturing practice. At present, 14 types of food have been listed in this category.

2. Standardized foods: Food produced under this category must adhere to quality standards as defined in the regulations. This category was created to standardize the production of locally produced food from small-scale or household industries in order to provide consumers the ability to differentiate such products by qualitative attributes and encourage food producers on attaining hygienic quality of their products. Standardized foods do not require registration and consists of 31 food types.

3. Food required to bear standardized labels: This category is less-restrictive than the first two categories, as food under this category pose a lower risk to consumers' health and does not have to follow specific quality standards for its manufacturing. However, products must bear standardized labels that provide consumer information. There are 13 food items in this category.

4. General foods: Consists of raw, cooked, preserved, non-preserved, processed or non-processed foods that are not listed in the above categories. Although registrations are not required, general food products are controlled and monitored based on hygiene, safety, labeling and advertisements.

The latest food category table can be found in GAIN report TH8116.

The following food production categories are also subject to additional regulations. These include quality standards for food containers, plastic containers, and feeding bottles.

1.2 Prohibited Food and Substances

1. Substances prohibited in foods:
- Brominated vegetable oil
- Salicylic acid
- Boric acid
- Borax
- Calcium iodate or potassium iodate except to be used to adjust the nutrition that related to iodine deficiency as approved by the Food and Drug Administration.
- Nitrofurazone
- Potassium chlorate
- Formaldehyde, formaldehyde solution and paraformaldehyde
- Coumarin, or 1,2-benzopyrone, or 5,6-benzo-alpha-pyrone, or cis-o-coumaric acid anhydride, or o-hydroxycinnamic acid, lactone
- Dihydrocoumarin, or benzodihydropyrone, or 3,4-dihydrocoumarin, or hydrocoumarin
- Methyl alcohol or methanol except for use as processing aids for export purpose.
- Diethyleneglycol, or dihydroxydiethyl ether, or diglycol, or 2,2'-oxybis-ethanol, or 2,2'-oxydiethanol

2. Foods prohibited to be manufactured, imported, or sold:

- Genetically modified food containing Cry9C DNA Sequence and food containing such genetically modified food.
- Ready-to-eat gelatin and jelly, which contain glucomannan or konjac flour packed in small containers with diameter or diagonal of the widest part not larger than 4.5 cm.
- All kinds of puffer fish and foods containing puffer fish meat as ingredients.
- Dulcin (para-phenetolcarbamide), which is used as sweetener.
- Cyclamic acid and its salts excluding salt of cyclamic acid which is sodium cyclamate.
- AF2 or furylframide, commonly called 2-(2-furyl)-3-(5-nitro-2-furyl) acrylamide as chemical name which used as food additive.
- Potassium bromate as food additive.
- Food containing dulcin, AF2 or Potassium bromate as a food ingredient.
- Food containing daminozide or succinic acid 2,2-dimetylhydrazide
- Stevia (scientific name as Stevia rebaudiana Bertoni) and its products except for production, import or sale of (1) Stevia leaf pursuant to the Notification of the Ministry of Public Health Re: Herbal Tea ; (2) Steviol glycoside pursuant to the Notification of the Ministry of Public Health Re: Food Additive No. 4-Steviol glycoside; (3) Stevia or its products used for production or such imported or sold for production of Steviol glycoside according to (2); (4) Stevia or its products produced for export.
- Modified milk for infants, modified milk in the form of follow up formula for infants and young children, infant food, food in the form of follow up formula for infants and young children, food and supplementary food for infants and young children containing melamine and its analogues (cyanuric acid) exceeding 1 mg/kg and other foods containing melamine and its analogues exceeding 2.5 mg/kg.

- Food containing objects other than food packed inside food packages, except for the purposes of food quality or standard preservation such as desiccator, oxygen absorber, etc., in separate packages, seasonings or consuming accessories (such as plastic spoon, chopsticks, measuring spoon, etc.) Objects other than food may be packed with the food packages, but only if they do not pose a risk to humans or mislead consumers that those objects can be eaten.

3. Food prohibited to be imported or sold:

3.1 Foods with expiration dates or suitable periods of consumption, which have lapsed as stated in the label:
- Infant food and food of continuous formula for infants and children.
- Supplementary food for infants and children.
- Modified food for infants and modified milk of continuous formula for infants and children
- Cultured milk
- Cow's milk that has been pasteurized, for example, pasteurized fresh milk, recombined pasteurized milk, flavored pasteurized milk and pasteurized milk products, etc.
- Food with special objectives.

3.2 Beef and beef products from Great Britain, Portugal, France, Ireland, Switzerland, Belgium, Germany, Netherlands, Denmark, Italy, Liechtenstein, Luxembourg, Spain, Czech Republic, Greece, Japan, Slovakia, Slovenia, Austria, Finland, Israel, Poland, Canada, and the United States; except milk and milk products, hides and skins, gelatin and collagen prepared from hides and skins and bone, protein-free tallow, dicalcium phosphate, deboned skeletal muscle meat and its products from cattle 30 months of age or less, and blood and blood by-products (see more details in item 6.6 of Section 6).

1.3 Regulatory Procedures

While some of the following information does not specifically apply to U.S. exporters, the following will be levied upon importers of U.S. products. The principles of regulatory procedures for food involve the following aspects.

1.3.1 Pre-marketing Control

Activities at this stage are the responsibility of the Food Bureau in the FDA.

(A) Establishing food standards and manufacturing requirements:
Food manufacturing standards and practices must meet the minimum acceptable requirements as established by the Subcommittee on Food Standards and Local Manufacturing Requirements.

(B) Food manufacturing licensing:
Local food manufacturers intending to sell their products must apply for a license prior to being operational. Plant layouts must be submitted for approval to the Thai FDA's Food Bureau. The FDA inspectors will then visit and inspect the plant before a manufacturing license can be issued. It is the responsibility of the licensee to renew the license every three years.

(C) Food importation licensing:

A license is required for importing food for sale in the country. FDA inspectors will visit and examine the suitability of the designated storage facility or warehouse before a license is issued. A licensee may import various kinds of food provided that the Office of Food and Drug Administration approves the food products. A license to import must be renewed every three years.

A temporary import license is needed for occasional import of food (i.e. for exhibition). An exemption will be granted only for the import of food samples for laboratory test and consideration for purchase.

(D) Food product registration:

Importers of food products deemed to be specifically-controlled food are required to register the products before importation for sale. However, exemptions are granted for products imported directly by food service outlets and manufacturers for their own use as ingredients or materials for food processing.

Applications for product registration should be submitted to the Food Bureau, FDA. For those residing outside the Bangkok Metropolitan area, applications can be submitted to the relevant Provincial Office of Public Health.

The approximate amount of time required for product registration, starting from submitting the application, is about one month. However, delays are usually caused by inaccurate or incomplete information, which is usually the basis for failing to register a product.

The details of applying for food product registration are provided in appendixes of the report; a flow chart of product registration is available in GAIN report.

(E) Food labeling:

Imported food products, which are categorized as specifically-controlled food, standardized foods, and foods are required to display labels according to the specific requisites of each category. Details on the label requirements are provided in Section 2.

(F) Nutrition labeling:

Nutrition labeling is required for some products. Details on the standard label requirements are discussed in Section 2.

(G) The requirement of Good Manufacturing Practices (GMP)

Under Ministerial Notification No. 193, B.E. 2543 (2000), Method of Food Manufacturing and Equipment for Manufacturing Food and Food Storage, Thailand requires domestic manufacturers and foreign suppliers of 57 types of products to adhere to GMP. These include:
- Infant food and follow-up formula food for infant and children
- Supplementary food for infant and children
- Modified milk for infant and follow-up formula modified milk for infant and children
- Ice
- Drinking water in sealed containers

- Beverage in sealed containers
- Food in sealed containers
- Cow's milk
- Cultured milk
- Ice cream
- Flavored milk
- Other milk products
- Food additives
- Food Colors
- Food enhancers
- Sodium cyclamate and food containing sodium cyclamate
- Food for weight control
- Tea
- Coffee
- Fish sauce
- Remaining solution from Mono Sodium Glutamate production
- Natural mineral water
- Vinegar
- Fat and oil
- Peanut oil
- Cream
- Butter oil
- Butter
- Cheese
- Ghee
- Margarine
- Semi-processed food
- Some particular kinds of sauces
- Palm oil
- Coconut oil
- Electrolyte drinks
- Soybean milk in sealed containers (except manufacturers which are not recognized as factory conforming to Factory Laws)
- Chocolate
- Jam, jelly, marmalade in sealed containers
- Food for special purpose
- Alkaline-preserved Eggs
- Royal jelly and Royal jelly products
- Products from the hydrolysis or fermentation of soybean protein
- Honey (except manufacturers which are not recognized as factory conforming to Factory Laws)
- Fortified rice with vitamins
- Husked rice flour
- Brine for cooking
- Sauce in sealed containers

- Bread
- Gum and candy
- Processed gelatin and jelly desserts
- Foods packed together with material intended for quality control purposes
- Garlic products
- Some Meat Products
- Flavoring Agents
- Foods containing Aloe Vera
- Frozen foods

Domestic manufacturers of these products must comply with the requirements outlined in the Ministerial Notification. Meanwhile, importers of the covered products must present an equivalent certificate of GMP for factories or plants that manufacture those products in line with the Thai GMP Law. The acceptable GMP can be any of the following: a) GMP by Thai Law; b) GMP by Codex; c) HACCP; d) ISO 9000; and e) other practice equivalent to (a)-(d).

For U.S. food products, Thai FDA officials agree that U.S. practices (it is understood that all U.S. food manufacturers are already subject to 21CFR part 110) exceed GMP criteria under the present Thai GMP Law. Accordingly, any simple statement/certificate (including HACCP certificate) that is endorsed by U.S. Government (USG) agencies will be acceptable. The statement may state that "the food product(s) are manufactured by U.S. processing plant(s), which are subject to 21CFR part 110." In 2010, the Thai FDA accepted the FSIS Form 9060-5 Meat and Poultry Export Certificate of Wholesomeness as a GMP certificate equivalent and must include the following statement, "Products were manufactured in accordance with the Food Safety and Inspection Service (FSIS) Hazard Analysis Critical Point (HACCP) regulatory requirement."

On November 7, 2012 the Thai Food and Drug Administration established GMP measures to cover other prepackaged food products (besides the 57 products previously mentioned) aimed to reduce primary contamination, prevent cross contamination, and eliminate physical, chemical, and biological hazards. U.S. exporters of other prepackaged food must provide Thai importers a certificate stating it meets the GMP requirements as stipulated in Ministry of Public Health Notification No. 342 B.E. 2555 (2012). In addition to the Ministerial Notification No. 193 and No. 342, the Thai FDA also set specific GMP guidelines that both local and foreign food manufacturers are required to comply with. This rule applies to the specific products listed below.

- Drinking water in sealed container (Ministerial Notification No. 220 / 2544 (2001) Re: Drinking Water in Sealed Containers).
- Pasteurized ready-to-consumed milk products (Ministerial Notification No.298 B.E.2549 (2006) Re: Production Processes, Production Equipments, and storage of ready-to-be-consumed milk products in liquid form which passed through pasteurization heat treatment).
- Irradiated food (Ministerial Notification No.297 B.E.2549 Re: Irradiated Food).
- Low acid and acidified foods in sealed containers (Ministerial Notification No.349 B.E.2555 Re: Production methods, tools and equipment used in the production, and food storage for low acid and acidified foods in sealed containers. (Additional information and specific certificate requirement are available in Gain report TH4128 re: Processing Filing for Low-Acid and Acidified Certificate Required)

1.3.2 Post-marketing Control

  A. Compliance Monitoring:

Monitoring processes primarily ensure that the food produced is wholesome and complies with the national food standards. Inspection of food factories and premises throughout the country are regularly conducted together with sampling of food products for laboratory testing. Technical guidance on the appropriate food production, delivery, handling and storage are also given during the monitoring process. If violations occur, product recall and prosecution will be executed. Inspection, monitoring, and legal actions are the responsibility of the Thai FDA's Inspection Division.

  B. Food surveillance:
The aim of the program is to assure the safety and quality of food distributed throughout the country. The aim of food surveillance is to assure the safety and quality of food items distributed in the market place. Food surveillance is conducted mainly by the Thai FDA. Its inspectors will take samples of food in markets from time to time and whenever problems are identified. The samples will be delivered to the Food Analysis Division of the Department of Medical Science for further analysis of toxins, pesticide residues, heavy metals, nutritional values, and standard conformity. Warning and legal actions such as seizures, product recalls, etc., will be taken depending on the degree of violation.

1.3.3 Advertisement

Any form of food advertisement through any public media is subject to approval from the FDA. False or misleading advertising on the quality or benefit claims are prohibited. The FDA's Advertisement Control and Public Relations Division is responsible for the approval of statements and visual images used in food advertising.

Section II. Labeling Requirements:
2.1 Standard Labeling

Imported food products or domestic food products are required to display labels. For imported foods, a Thai label must be applied where needed prior to entry and be affixed to every single item of food product prior to marketing. Failure to apply the label before entry will lead to product seizure by the FDA. The Thai FDA only requires pre-approved labels for specifically-controlled foods. For other foods, the food manufacturers or food importers are responsible to prepare a product label that complies with the Ministerial Notification No. 367 B.E. 2557 Re: Food Labeling of Prepackaged Food, which is the new food labeling law for all prepackaged foods that became effective on December 3, 2014. (See GAIN report TH4091)

2.1.1 Labeling of Food Products Sold Directly to Consumers

Labels for food products sold directly to consumers shall be in the Thai language and shall have the following details, except for those exempted by the FDA:

1. Food name

2. Food serial number

3. Name and addresses of producers, or re-packers, or importer, or headquarters as the case may be, as follows:

    (3.1) For foods manufactured in the country, it is required to display name and address of the manufacturer, or repacker, or name and address of headquarters of the manufacturer or repacker with following information:

        (3.1.1) the term "Manufacturer" or "Manufactured by" in case of the manufacturer;

        (3.1.2) the term "Repacker" or "Repacked by" in case of the repacker;

        (3.1.3) the term "Headquarters" in case of displaying address of headquarters of the manufacturer or repacker.

    (3.2) For imported foods, it is required to display name and address of importer with the term "Importer" or "Imported by" and also the name and country of the manufacturer.

4. Food quantities shall be expressed in the metric system:

    (4.1) Food in solid form shall be expressed in net weight;

    (4.2) Foods in liquid form shall be expressed in net volume;

    (4.3) Foods in semi-solid form may be expressed either in net weight or net volume;

    For foods required to set drained weight according to the Notification of the Ministry of Public Health, it is required to display such drained weight.

5. Ingredients presented in estimated weight percentage in descending order except:

    (5.1) Foods with the whole label area less than 35 cm2, but it is required to contain information showing ingredients on their packaging or

    (5.2) Foods containing only single ingredients irrespective of food additives or flavoring agent.

    (5.3) For dried or powdered or concentrated foods needed to be diluted or dissolved before being consumed, it may choose to display either major ingredients in estimated percentage or components when diluted or dissolved by means of preparing as indicated on the label or display both.

6. Message "Information for food allergy: contains………….." in case using as ingredients or "information for food allergy: may contain……………." in case of possible contamination during manufacturing process, as the case may be (blank area shall be filled with type or kind of allergen) where the font pattern shall be in accordance with Clause 14(3) of the notification and font color in contrast to the label background, font size not less than that of displaying the ingredients, and shown at the lower part of ingredients presentation.

    Type or kind of food, which is an allergen or substance causing hypersensitivity includes:

    (6.1) cereal grain containing gluten (e.g. wheat, rye, barley, oat, spelt or hybrid strain of those cereal grain and the products thereof);

    (6.2) crustacean and products of these (e.g. crab, shrimp, Mantis shrimp, lobster);

    (6.3) egg and egg products;

    (6.4) fish and fish products;

    (6.5) peanut, soybean and peanut and soybean products;

    (6.6) milk and dairy products (including lactose);

    (6.7) tree nuts and nuts products (e.g. almond, walnut, pecan); and

    (6.8) sulphide of 10 mg/kg or above.

However, it does not include food that the allergen or substances causing hypersensitivity are major ingredients and clearly state the allergen or substances causing hypersensitivity in the food name such as fresh cow's milk, crispy roasted peanut, etc.

7. Display name of the food additive group with specific name or display food additive group together with the International Numbering System (INS) pursuant to the Notification of the Ministry of Public Health regarding Food Additives. A food additive carried over into a food in a significant quantity or in an amount sufficient to perform a technological function in that food as a result of the use of raw materials or other ingredients in which the additive was used shall also display the following messages as the case may be:

(7.1) "Natural colors" or "Synthetic colors" followed by specific name or INS number (as the case may be); and

(7.2) Group name followed by specific name for flavor enhancer and sweetener.

8. Declarations of "Natural flavor, Identical natural flavor or Artificial flavor" as the applicable case.

9. Declarations of "date, month and year" for foods with shelf life not exceeding 90 days or declarations of "date, month and year" or "month and year" for foods with shelf life exceeding 90 days with declaration of "Best Before."

In addition, the declaration of "manufacture or expire" may be required subject to the notification of the Ministry of Public Health regarding such foods.

Declaration of "date, month and year" or "month and year" shall be in order of "date, month and year" or "month and year" and "month" may be indicated in number or alphabet. Otherwise, it is required to have the information clearly comprehensible by the consumer of such declaration format. 10. Warning (if any).

11. Instruction for food storage (if any).

12. Food preparation method for consumption (if any).

13. Instruction for use and necessary instruction for foods intended for infant or young children or any particular group.

14. Additional declarations prescribed as per the schedule attached hereto.

15. Declarations required for foods prescribed under the notification of the Ministry of Public Health.

2.1.2 Labeling of Food Products Sold to Food Manufacturers as Ingredients (also refer to Section 2.8 Food Additive Labeling). Information below is required to be displayed:

1. Food name

2. Food serial number

3. Name and addresses of producers, or re-packers, or importer, or headquarters, as the case may be, as follows:

(3.1) For foods manufactured in the country, it is required to display name and address of manufacturer, or repacker, or name and address of headquarters of manufacturer or repacker with following information:

(3.1.1) the term "Manufacturer" or "Manufactured by" in case of the manufacturer;

(3.1.2) the term "Repacker" or "Repacked by" in case of the repacker;

(3.1.3) the term "Headquarters" in case of displaying address of headquarters of the manufacturer or repacker.

(3.2) For imported foods, it is required to display name and address of importer with the term "Importer" or "Imported by" and also the name and country of manufacturer.

4. Food quantities shall be expressed in the metric system:

(4.1) Food in solid form shall be expressed in net weight;

(4.2) Foods in liquid form shall be expressed in net volume;

(4.3) Foods in semi-solid form may be expressed either in net weight or net volume;

For foods required to set drained weight according to the Notification of the Ministry of Public Health, it is required to display such drained weight.

5. Ingredients presented in estimated weight percentage in descending order except:

(5.1) Foods with the whole label area less than 35 cm2, but it is required to contain information showing ingredients on their packaging or

(5.2) Foods containing only single ingredients irrespective of food additives or flavoring agent.

(5.3) For dried or powdered or concentrated foods needed to be diluted or dissolved before being consumed, it may choose to display either major ingredients in estimated percentage or components when diluted or dissolved by means of preparing as indicated on the label or display both.

6. Declarations of "date, month and year" for foods with shelf life not exceeding 90 days or declarations of "date, month and year" or "month and year" for foods with shelf life exceeding 90 days with declaration of "Best Before."

In addition the declaration of "manufacture" or "expire" may be required subject to the notification of the Ministry of Public Health regarding such foods.

Declaration of "date, month and year" or "month and year" shall be in order of "date, month and year" or "month and year" and "month" may be indicated in number or alphabet. Otherwise, it is required to have the information clearly comprehensible by the consumer of such declaration format. The information (1-6) may be expressed in English on the label provided that complete details in Thai are always expressed as required in such a clear and easy to read manner in the manual or sale documents.

2.1.3 Labeling of Modified Milk for Infants

In order to promote the importance of maternal milk and the benefits received from drinking maternal milk for both infants and small children, the Thai FDA requires producers and importers of modified milk and modified milk of uniform formula for infant and children to display the following statements on the label:

- The best food for infants is maternal milk owing to its full nutritional content.
- Modified milk for infants should be recommended by a physician, nurse or nutritionist.
- Incorrect preparation or mixture will be hazardous for infants.

2.1.4 Labeling of Cow's Milk

Exporters must follow new labeling requirements stated under the Ministry of Public Health Notification No. 350 Re: Cow's Milk that govern the display and declaration statements of certain types of cow's milk on food labels. However, for other general labeling requirements, the exporter can refer to the Ministry of Public Health Notification No. 194 Re: Food Labels (See GAIN report TH2111).

2.1.5 The Use of the Term "Premium" on Food Labels

The Thai Food and Drug Administration (FDA) requires food manufacturers or importers of products which use the term "premium" on their products' labels to meet a certain set of quality, standards, and specific characteristics as stipulated under Ministry of Public Health Notification No. 365 Re: Expression of the term "Premium" on food labels. To export products that display the term "premium" on food labels, an exporter must submit the required documents to the Thai Food and Drug

Administration to prove that their products meet the criteria listed in the notification. (See GAIN report TH3099).

2.2 Nutrition Labeling

The regulations on nutrition labeling are based on the Ministerial Notification No. 182 of B.E. 2541. (1998) and No. 219 of B.E. 2544 (2001). Nutritional labeling is mandatory for the following types of food.
- Foods making a specific nutritional claim.
- Foods that make use of nutritional values in sale promotions.
- Foods that specifically target a group of consumers (e.g. students, executives, elderly people, etc.)
- Other foods which may be specified by the FDA including potato chips, corn chips, extruded snack foods, biscuits/crackers, assorted wafers as per Ministerial Notification No. 305. Effective as of December 18, 2007 the Thai FDA requires nutrition labeling for five groups of processed foods by displaying information that states "Should take less and exercise for a better health." Details of the notification are discussed in GAIN Report TH7136.

Exemptions of these nutrition-labeling regulations (as defined in Ministerial Notification No. 182) are infant foods, supplementary foods for infants and children, and other types of food for which labeling requirements have been otherwise regulated; food not directly sold to consumers; and food packed in small containers which will be repacked and sold in a larger container. Nutrition labeling must be presented in Thai and a foreign language is optional. The standard U.S. nutrition fact panel is not acceptable as Thai Recommended Daily Intakes may not be identical to the United States. In addition, differences may exist in serving size and reference amount.

Depending upon the labeling space, different formats are applicable, on either a vertical or horizontal basis. An example of standard comprehensive nutrition facts is provided. The format is similar to the U.S. nutrition fact panel but not identical.

Nutrition Facts

Serving Size: ....
Servings Per Container....:....

Amount Per Serving
Total Calories ....kcal (Calories from Fat .... kcal)

		% Recommended Daily Intakes *
Total Fat	..........g	..... %
Saturated Fat	..........g	.....%
Cholesterol	..........mg	.....%
Protein	..........g	.....%
Total Carbohydrate	..........g	.....%
Dietary Fiber	..........g	.....%
Sugars	..........g	..... %
Sodium	..........mg	..... %

% Recommended Daily Intakes *

Vitamin A	..... %	**Vitamin B1**	.... %
Vitamin B2	..... %	**Calcium**	.... %
Iron	..... %		

* Percent recommended daily intakes are based on a 2,000 kcal diet for Thais aged six and upwards.

Individual calorie needs may differ. Based on a 2,000 kcal daily diet, the nutrient intakes shall be as follows.

Total Fat	Less than	65 g
Saturated Fat	Less than	20 g
Cholesterol	Less than	300 mg
Total Carbohydrate		300 g
Dietary Fiber		25 g
Sodium	Less than	2,400 mg

Calories (kcal) per gram: Fat = 9; Protein = 4; Carbohydrate = 4

Details on serving size and servings per container may be omitted where the reference on serving size cannot be determined due to the nature of that food. Hence, instead of the statement "amount per serving", the statement "amount per 100 g" or "amount per 100 ml" shall be used as appropriate.

Guideline Daily Amounts (GDA) Labeling

As of August 2011 the Thai FDA requires five groups of snack foods to label the Guideline Daily Amounts (GDA) on the front of the product's package including fried or baked potato chips, fried or baked popcorn, rice crisps or extruded snacks, crackers or biscuits, and filling wafers–. The GDA label must include the nutritional value of the product and the recommended daily consumption regarding energy, sugar, fat, and sodium. The format of the label is the following:

Nutritional value per………
Consumption should be split into …………times.

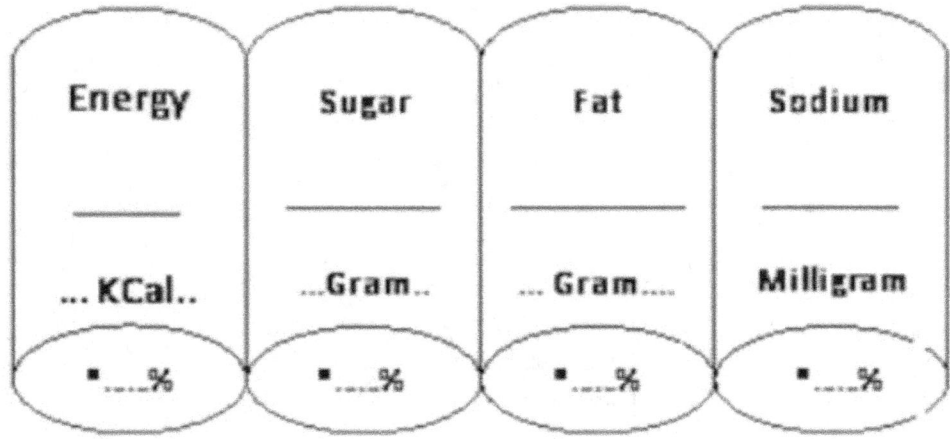

*Percentage of maximum consumption volume allowed per day

More details on the GDA labeling format and requirements are available in GAIN report TH1077.

2.3 Thai Recommended Daily Intakes (Thai RDIs)

The Thai Recommended Daily Intake (Thai RDIs) for people of six years of age and older are the established guidelines for nutritional labeling. The Thai Recommended Daily Dietary Allowances (Thai RDA) were developed using as reference the U.S. RDA and Codex's Nutrient Reference Values, details on Thai RDIs are provided below.

No.	Nutrient	Thai RDI	Unit
1	Total Fat	65*	Gram
2	Saturated Fat	20*	Gram
3	Cholesterol	300	Milligram
4	Protein	50*	Gram
5	Total Carbohydrate	300*	Gram
6	Dietary Fiber	25	Gram
7	Vitamin A	800 (2,664)	Microgram RE (IU)
8	Thiamin	1.5	Milligram
9	Riboflavin	1.7	Milligram

10	Niacin	20	Milligram NE
11	Vitamin B6	2	Milligram
12	Folic Acid	200	Microgram
13	Biotin	150	Microgram
14	Pantothenic Acid	6	Milligram
15	Vitamin B12	2	Microgram
16	Vitamin C	60	Milligram
17	Vitamin D	5 (200)	Microgram (IU)
18	Vitamin E	10 (15)	Milligram Alpha TE (IU)
19	Vitamin K	80	Microgram
20	Calcium	800	Milligram
21	Phosphorus	800	Milligram
22	Iron	15	Milligram
23	Iodine	150	Microgram
24	Magnesium	350	Milligram
25	Zinc	15	Milligram
26	Copper	2	Milligram
27	Potassium	3,500	Milligram
28	Sodium	2,400	Milligram
29	Manganese	3.5	Milligram
30	Selenium	70	Microgram
31	Fluoride	2	Milligram
32	Molybdenum	160	Microgram
33	Chromium	130	Microgram
34	Chloride	3,400	Milligram

Notes:
1. * RDIs for total fat, saturated fat, protein and total carbohydrate are 30, 10, 10 and 60 respectively of the total daily calories (2,000 kilocalories).
2. Sugar intake should not be more than 10% of the total daily calories.

2.4 Claims

2.4.1 Nutritional Claims

A nutritional claim means any presentation which states, suggests or implies that a food has particular nutritional properties including, but not limited, to the caloric value, the content of protein, fat and carbohydrates, as well as the content of vitamins and minerals. Nutritional claims constitute nutrient content claims, comparative claims and nutrient function claims.

The Thai FDA generally uses Codex and U.S. FDA standards as guidelines to develop their own nutritional claims guidelines, as such the descriptors used in nutrient content claim (e.g. low in cholesterol) and comparative claims (e.g. "less", "reduced") generally have similar definitions to those used in the U.S. for food labeling. However, there may be some differences in the use of certain terms such as "good source" or "rich in" as the threshold values for nutrients might be greater than what is used in the US to be able to make such claims and differences may also exist in serving sizes and recommended daily intakes. Further details can be obtained from the Thai FDA's Food Bureau.

(A) Nutrient content claims are a nutrition claim that described the level of nutrient contained in a food. Examples are "source of calcium, high in fiber and low in fat," etc. A food that is by its nature low in or free of the nutrient that is the subject of the claim shall not include the term "low" or "free" in the name of the food. Instead, a claim statement may be made in a general form that refers of all foods of that type (e.g. vegetable oil) are cholesterol-free foods. However, foods that have been specially processed, altered, formulated or reformulated so as to lower the amount of nutrient in the food or remove the nutrient from the food may bear such a claim.

(B) Comparative claims are claims that compare the nutrient levels and/or energy value of two or more foods. Examples are "less than, fewer, more than, reduced, lite/light," etc. Comparative claims can be made if the foods being compared or "reference foods" are different versions of the same food or similar foods that are representative of the same type available in the market. The identity of the reference food shall be given and a statement of the amount difference in the nutrient content or energy value shall be expressed as a percentage or fraction, higher or lower than that of the food being compared. Also, the nutrient content per serving shall be provided. Full details of the comparison are needed.

Comparative claims are not allowed in the case where reference foods already contain "low" or "very low" levels of nutrient content or energy values according to the established conditions defined in Appendix 4 of the Ministerial Notification No. 182 (B.E. 2541) Re: Nutrition Labeling.

(C) Nutrient function claims are claims relating to the function of a nutrient in the body. Examples are "calcium aids in the development of strong bones and teeth" and "Iron is a factor in red blood cell formation." Nutrient function claims are subject to FDA approval and are permitted provided the following conditions are met.
- Only those essential nutrients listed in the Thai RDIs shall be the subject of a nutrient function claim.
- The food for which the claim is made shall be a significant source of the nutrient in the diet.
- The claim must be made with reference to the nutrient not particularly to the food product.
- The claim must be based on reliable scientific evidence.
- The claim must not imply or include any statement to the effect that the nutrient would afford a cure or treatment for or protection from disease.

2.4.2 Health Claims

A health claim means any presentation which states, suggests or implies that a food or nutrient in the food has anything to do with disease or health condition. As many factors (i.e. sex, age, heredity, etc.) can be causes of disease for an individual, no health claim is therefore allowed on food products in Thailand.

2.5 GMO Labeling

The Thai government has banned the commercial planting of transgenic crops, but does allow imports of transgenic soybeans and corn for a wide-range of domestic uses in both the feed milling and food processing industries. On May 11, 2003 the Ministry of Public Health implemented the labeling law for food containing Genetically Modified Organisms (GMO) materials/products. The regulations claiming to protect consumers were apparently based on the Japanese model allowing for a 5 percent tolerance.

The products covered by this law are listed as follows:
- Soybeans
- Cooked soybean
- Roasted soybean
- Bottled or canned soybean or soybean contained in retort pouch
- Natto (fermented soybean)
- Miso
- Tofu or Tofu fried in oil
- Frozen tofu, soybean gluten from tofu or its products
- Soybean milk
- Soybean flour
- Food containing product(s) from (1) to (10) as main ingredient
- Food containing soybean protein as main ingredient
- Food containing green soybean as main ingredient
- Food containing soybean sprout as main ingredient
- Corn
- Popcorn
- Frozen or chilled corn
- Bottled or canned corn or corn contained in retort pouch
- Corn flour or corn starch
- Snack deriving from corn as main ingredient
- Food containing product(s) from (15) to (20) as main ingredient
- Food containing corn grits as main ingredient

GMO labeling is required for any processed product containing recombinant DNA or protein resulting from gene technology over 5 percent of each top three main ingredients by weight and each ingredient constitutes over 5 percent of the total product weight.

Product labeling by the producer/importer is mandatory, products that do not adhere to the regulation may be confiscated and the producer/importer will be subject to the applicable penalties if found at fault. More details about GMO labeling procedures are provided in the Manual for Labeling Procedures for GMO Products according to the Ministerial Notification No. 251, B.E. 2545 (2002).

2.6 Irradiated Food Imports to Thailand

Effective as of October 2010 irradiated food manufacturers and importers must ensure that irradiated food manufactured or sold in Thailand must be labeled in accordance with the requirements prescribed in the Ministry of Public Health Notification Re: Irradiated Food (2553/2010). The regulation requires the labeling of irradiated food to display the symbol of food irradiation and the wording "irradiated" to be adjacent to the name of food or any irradiated food ingredient under the ingredient list. In addition, importers of irradiated foods must provide a certificate of the establishment for irradiation processing as prescribed in the Ministerial Notification or the equivalent form from the government authorities or other accepted documents by the government of the countries of origin. More information on the requirements is available in GAIN report TH0075).

2.7 Iodized Salt Labeling

Under the government's Universal Salt Iodization (USI) strategy, the FDA requires edible salts (including table salt and salt used as food ingredients) to be iodized in order to reduce the iodine deficiency in children and pregnant woman in Thailand. For table salt, iodine must not be less than 30 mg/kg of edible salt and the wording "Iodized Edible Salt" has to be displayed adjacent to the name of the food product. For any product containing salt as an ingredient, the wording of "Iodized Edible Salt" is also required under the ingredient list. The Thai FDA also requires the following information, "For people who need to limit iodine consumption" on products that that contain non-iodized salt.

2.8 Food Additive Labeling

The labeling of food additives must have text in the Thai language (may accompany foreign text). It must contain clear and readable details as follows:
(1) Name of food, marked by the word "food additives" or functional classes.
(2) Food serial number.
(3) Name and address of manufacturer or packer of food additives produced in the country. For imported food additives, the display of name and address of importer and producing country is required. However, for food additives produced in the country, the name and the headquarter address of food additive manufacturer or packer can be used instead.
(4) Lot identification by the word "Lot No." or marked with other text that can be used for product traceability.
(5) The net contents shall be declared in metric measurements.
    (5.1) for solid food additives, by net weight;
    (5.2) for liquid food additives, by net volume;
    (5.3) for semi-solid food additives, either by net weight or net volume;
    (5.4) for food additives are in form of tablet or capsule, by net weight and number of tablets must be shown.
(6) Month and year of manufacture or month and year of expiration must be labeled accordingly to "manufactured on (specify month and year)" or "expired on (specify month and year)" or similar text. Food additives with a shelf-life less than 18 months must display the expiry date and year using the text as "expired on (specify month and year)" or other information that provide the same meaning such as "can be used until (specify month and year)."
(7) The food components must display food additive components and other food ingredients as follows:

    (7.1) For food additive components, the common name of food additives must be shown. In addition, the quantity of food additives must be given in percentage and listed by weight in descending order. The common name of notification of food additives must be shown in a specific name, according to CODEX's general standard for food additives or the Ministry of Public Health on Food additives. Numbers must be provided and be in accordance with International Numbering System (INS) for food additives.

For food additives sold to food manufacturers to be used as materials for their further processing and not sold directly to consumers, or food additives sold to packers, only food additive names with International Numbering System (INS) are required to be displayed. The name listed by weight in descending order.

(7.2) For other food ingredients, the name of food ingredients must be declared in the list of ingredients in descending order of proportion.

In case other food ingredients contain flavoring agents, instead of displaying the flavoring agents' names, the following information may be used: "contains flavoring agents, contains natural flavoring agents, contains natural flavoring agent imitations or contains artificial flavoring agents." In case other food ingredients contain spices or herbs, the wording "spice" or "herb" can be used in lieu of their names. However, this does not apply to flavor modifiers.

(8) The usage instruction must be given and at least cover the following:

    (8.1) Usage objective.

    (8.2) Food type.

    (8.3) Amount of food additive used in food.

(9) Instructions for storage.

(10) Restrictions on use and warnings or cautions (if any).

The displayed text under (1) (5) and (6) must be in the position that can be clearly seen. In case a display of the information of (6) is shown at the bottom of the container, the text must clearly indicate how to find the information as per (6).

For food additive, which is produced and imported to be sold to food manufacturers as materials for further processing and not sold directly to consumers as well as those food additives sold to packers, the displayed text under (1) (2) (3) (4) (5) and (6) are required on the label with the text of "Only use as materials for food processing" or other information that carry the same meaning. The information can be displayed in English. However, if the quantity of food additives are displayed in percentage, the phrase "only use as materials for food processing" can be omitted and the information of (1)-(10) in Thai can be provided in the manual or sales documents.

(11) Labeling of food additives produced for export can be displayed in any language, but at the minimum required to provide the following information:

    (1) Name of producing countries.

    (2) Food serial number or the identification of the producing factory.

    (3) Lot identification by the word "Lot No." or marked with other text that can be traceable.

Section III. Packaging and Container Regulations:

The Thai FDA requires that all packaging and containers of food must comply with Ministerial Notification No. 92, B.E. 2528 (1985) and No. 295, B.E. 2548 (2005). The guidelines on packaging and containers are as follows:

(A) A container must:

- Be clean.

- Not emit any heavy metal or other substances that would contaminate food in a volume to be harmful

to health.
- Free of germ contamination.
- Emit no food contaminating color.

(B) Containers which are made from ceramic or enameled metal must conform to subsection (A) and meet lead and cadmium standards as described in Schedule 2 of the Ministerial Notification No. 92 (B.E. 2528) Re: Prescription of Quality or Standard for Food Containers, Use of Food Containers, and Prohibition of Use of Things as Food Containers.

(C) Containers which are made of plastic must conform to not only the quality or standard in subsection (A), but also the quality or standard in Schedule 1 of the Ministerial Notification No. 92 (B.E. 2528) Re: Prescription of Quality or Standard for Food Containers, Use of Food Containers, and Prohibition of Use of Things as Food Containers.

(D) Plastics in the form of sheets or bags which are used as food containers must not be made from used plastic and must not have coloring except for: a) laminate plastic, only the layer that's not in direct contact with the food; and b) plastic which is used for packing shelled fruits.

(E) Plastic containers of milk, milk products, and other products similar to milk products (such as soybean milk and coconut milk) must be made from Polyethylene, Ethylene, 1-Alkene Copolymerized resin, Polypropylene, Polystyrene or Polyethyleneterephthalate.

(F) Use of containers that have previously been used to pack or wrap fertilizers, hazardous substance or any substance likely to be harmful to humans is prohibited.

(G) Use of containers that have been made to pack other products, which are not food, that bear a design or statement that may mislead to the actual contents of a particular food is prohibited.

Ministerial Notification No. 310, B.E. 2551 (2008) lists additional measures prohibiting objects other than food to be packed into food packaging (See GAIN report TH8082). The major revision of this notification is as follows:

- Objects other than food shall not be packed inside food packages, except for the purposes of food quality or standard preservation such as desiccators, oxygen absorber, etc., in separate packages; seasonings or consuming accessories (such as plastic spoon, chopsticks, measuring spoon, etc.).
- Objects other than food may be packed with the food packages, but only if they do not pose a risk to humans or mislead consumers that those objects can be eaten.

Section IV. Food Additives Regulations:
Food additives are substances which normally are not used as food or essential ingredients of food, whether or not such substances have food value, but which are added for the benefits of production technology, packing, storage or improve the quality or standards or the nature of food. They also include the substances mixed with food for the purposes stated earlier.

Food additives are specified as specifically-controlled food of which the quality or standards are defined. Use of food additives must follow the set objectives for specified kinds of food and maximum

permissible quantity, food additive functional classes categorized according to CODEX as listed below:
- Acid
- Acidity regulator
- Anticaking agent
- Antifoaming agent
- Antioxidant
- Bulking agent
- Color
- Color retention agent
- Emulsifier
- Emulsifying salt
- Firming agent
- Flavor enhancer
- Flour treatment agent
- Foaming agent
- Gelling agent
- Glazing agent
- Humectant
- Preservative
- Propellant
- Raising agent
- Stabilizer
- Sweetener
- Thickener

Use of food additives for purposes other than stated must be petitioned for the FDA's approval. Any food additives not listed below, but are available under CODEX (GSFA) are generally acceptable by the Thai FDA.

The list of permitted food additives in Thailand are provided below:
- Hydrochloric acid (INS 507)
- Sorbic acid (INS 200)
- Citric acid (INS 330)
- Thiodipropionic acid (INS 388)
- Benzoic acid (INS 210)
- Propionic acid (INS 280)
- Trans-butenedioic acid (INS 297)
- Phosphoric acid (INS 338)
- Formic acid (INS 236)
- Malic acid (INS 296)
- Lactic acid (INS 270)
- Acetic acid (INS 260)
- Algenic acid (INS 400)
- Glutamic acid (INS 620)

- L-tartaric acid (INS 334)
- L-ascorbic acid (INS 300)
- Isoascorbic acid (INS 315)
- Guanylic acid (INS 626)
- Inosinic acid (INS 630)
- Glucono-delta-lactone (INS 575)
- Glycerin (INS 422)
- Ester gum (INS 445)
- Salts of oleic acid (INS 470)
- Salts of myristic acid (INS 470)
- Ammonium salts of phosphatidic acid (INS 442)
- Karaya gum (INS 416)
- Guar gum (INS 412)
- Guaiac resin (INS 314)
- Gamma-cyclodextrin (INS 458)
- Beewax (INS 901)
- Carnauba wax (INS 903)
- Carbon dioxide (INS 290)
- Carmoisine (INS 122)
- Carotene (natural) (INS 160aii)
- Carrageenan (INS 407)
- Carob bean gum (INS 410)
- Curdlan (INS 424)
- Candelilla wax (INS 902)
- Canthaxanthin (INS161g)
- Ammonia caramel (INS 150c)
- Caustic caramel (INS 150a)
- Sulfite ammonia caramel (INS 150d)
- Calcium guanylate (INS 629)
- Calcium ribonucleotides (INS 634)
- Calcium inosinate (INS 633)
- Calcium gluconate (INS 578)
- Calcium chloride (INS 509)
- Calcium sulfate calcium glutamate (INS 623)
- Calcium carbonate (INS 170i)
- Calcium citrate (INS 333)
- Calcium silicate (INS 552)
- Calcium sorbate (INS 203)
- Calcium disodium (ethylenedinitrilo) (INS 385)
- Calcium DL-malate (INS 352ii)
- Calcium benzoate (INS 213)
- Calcium propionate (INS 282)
- Calcium ferrocyanide (INS 538)
- Calcium phosphate, dibasic (INS 341ii)

- Calcium phosphate, tribasic (INS 341ii)
- Calcium phosphate, monobasic (INS 341i)
- Calcium bisulphate (INS 227)
- Calcium lactate (INS 327)
- Calcium stearate (INS 470)
- Calcium oxide (INS 529)
- Calcium aluminium silicate (INS 556)
- Calcium acetate (INS 263)
- Calcium alginate (INS 404)
- Calcium ascorbate (INS 302)Calcium hydroxide (INS 526)
- Chlorine (INS 925)
- Chlorine dioxide (INS 926)
- Chlorophyll copper complex (INS 141 ii)
- Carmines (INS 120)
- Edible gelatin Gellan gum (INS 418)
- Shellac (INS 901)
- Sucrose acetate isobutyrate (INS 444)
- Sorbitol (INS 420)
- Sorbitan tristearate (INS 492)
- Sorbitan monopalmitate (INS 495)
- Sorbitan monostearate (INS 491)
- Sunset yellow FCF (INS 110)
- Sulfur dioxide (INS 220)
- Silicon dioxide (INS 551)
- Xylitol (INS 967)
- Sodium gluconate (INS 576)
- Sodium carbonate (INS 500i)
- Sodium carboxymethyl cellulose (INS 466)
- Sodium carboxy-methyl cellulose, enzymatically hydrolysed (INS 469)
- Sodium sulfate (INS 514)
- Sodium sulphite (INS 221)
- Sodium sesquicarbonate (INS 500iii)
- Sodium citrate (INS 331iii)
- Sodium sorbate (INS 201)
- Sodium nitrate (INS 251)
- Sodium nitrite (INS 250)
- Sodium DL-malate (INS 350ii)
- Sodium dihydrogen citrate (INS 331i)
- Sodium phosphate, tribasic (INS 339iii)
- Sodium phosphate, dibasic (INS 339ii)
- Sodium Polyphosphate (INS 425i)
- Sodium phosphate, monobasic (INS 339i)
- Sodium propionate (INS 281)
- Sodium bicarbonate (INS 500ii)

- Sodium benzoate (INS 211)
- Sodium tripolyphosphate sodium ferrocyanide (INS 535)
- Sodium fumalate (INS 365)
- Sodium bisulfite (INS 222)
- Sodium metabisulfite (INS 223)
- Sodium lactate (INS 325)
- Sodium acetate (INS 262i)
- Sodium alumino silicate (INS 554)
- Sodium alginate (INS 401)
- Sodium L-tartrate (INS 335ii)
- Sodium L-ascorbate (INS 301)
- Sodium D-isoascorbate (INS 316)
- Sodium o-phenyl phenol (INS 232)
- Sodium hydroxide (INS 524)
- Sodium hydrogen malate D (INS 350i)
- Powdered cellulose (INS 460ii)
- Xanthan gum (INS 415)
- Dextrins (INS 1400)
- Triacetin (INS 1518)
- Triammonium citrate (INS 380)
- Triethyl citrate (INS 1505)
- Tripotassium citrate (INS 332ii)
- Trisodium citrate (INS 331iii)
- Titanium dioxide (INS 171)
- Distarch phosphate (INS 1412)
- Dilauryl thiodipropionate (INS 389)
- Dimethyl polysiloxane (INS 900)
- Dimethyl dicarbonate (INS 242)
- Dipotassium 5'-inosinate (INS 632)
- Dipotassium 5'-guanylate (INS 628)
- Disodium 5'-inosinate (INS 631)
- Disodium 5' ribonucleotide (INS 635)
- Disodium 5'-guanylate (INS 627)Dodecyl gallate (INS 312)
- Tartrazine (INS 102)
- Talcum (INS 553iii)
- Tara gum (INS 417)
- Tragacanth gum (INS 413)
- Thaumatin (INS 957)
- Tocopherol concentrate mixed (INS 307b)
- Tosom (INS 479)
- Nisin (INS 234)
- Nitrous oxide (INS 942)
- Beta-carotene (synthetic) (INS 160ai)
- Beta-apo-8'-caotenal (INS 160e)

- Beta-cyclodextrin (INS 459)
- Butylated hydroxytoluene (INS 321)
- Butylated hydroxyanisole (INS 320)
- Brilliant blue FCF (INS 133)
- Bleached starch (INS 1403)
- Ponceau 4 R (INS 124)
- Konjac flour (INS 425)
- Propane (INS 944)
- Propyl gallate (INS 310)
- Propyl paraben (INS 216)
- Propylene glycol (INS 1520)
- Propylene glycol alginate (INS 405)
- Propylene glycol esters of fatty acids (INS 477)
- Vegetable carbon (INS 153)
- Pectin (INS 440)
- Potassium gluconate (INS 577)
- Potassium chloride (INS 508)
- Potassium carbonate (INS 501i)
- Potassium sorbate (INS 202)
- Potassium sulfate (INS 515)
- Potassium sulfite (INS 225)
- Potassium citrate (INS 332ii)
- Potassium DL-malate (INS 351ii)Potassium dihydrogen citrate (INS 332i)
- Potassium nitrate (INS 252)
- Potassium nitrite (INS 249)
- Potassium benzoate (INS 212)
- Potassium bicarbonate (INS 501ii)
- Potassium bisulfite (INS 228)
- Potassium propionate (INS 283)
- Potassium ferrocyanide (INS 536)
- Potassium phosphate, dibasic (INS 340ii)
- Potassium phosphate, tribasic (INS 340iii)
- Potassium phosphate, monobasic (INS 340i)
- Potassium metabisulfite (INS 224)
- Potassium lactate (INS 326)
- Potassium acetate (INS 261)
- Potassium alginate (INS 402)
- Potassium L-tartrate (INS 336)
- Potassium ascorbate (INS 303)
- Potassium hydroxide (INS 525)
- Potassium hydrogen DL, malate (INS 351ii)
- Polyglycerol esters of fatty acids (INS 475)
- Polyglycitol syrup (INS 964)
- Polydextrose (INS 1200)

- Polyvinyl pyrrolidone (INS 1201)
- Insoluble polyvinyl pyrrolidone (INS 1202)
- Polyoxyethylene (20) sorbitan monostearate (INS 435)
- Polyoxyethylene (20) sorbitan monooleate (INS 433)
- Polyethylene glycol (INS 1521)
- Pimaricin (INS 235)
- Fast green FCF (INS 143)
- Ferric ammonium citrate (INS 381)
- Ferrous gluconate (INS 579)
- Ferrous lactate (INS 585)
- Phosphated distarch phosphate (INS 1413)
- Methyl cellulose (INS 461)
- Methylparaben (INS 218)Methyl ethyl cellulose (INS 465)
- Beta-apo-8'-carotenoic acid (INS 160f)
- Magnesium gluconate (INS 580)
- Magnesium carbonate (INS 504i)
- Magnesium chloride (INS 511)
- Magnesium silicate (synthetic) (INS 553i)
- Magnesium hydroxide carbonate (INS 504 ii)
- Magnesium DI-L glutamate (INS 625)
- Magnesium DL-lactate (INS 329)
- Magnesium stearate (INS 470)
- Magnesium oxide (INS 530)
- Magnesium hydroxide (INS 528)
- Mannitol (INS 421)
- Maltitol (INS 965)
- Microcryltalline cellulose (INS 460 i)
- Microcrystalline wax (INS 905ci)
- Monosodium glutamate (INS 621)
- Monopotassium glutamate (INS 622)
- Mono and diglycerides (INS 471)
- Citric acid esters of mono- and diglycerides (INS 472c)
- Diacetyltartaric acid esters of mono- and diglycerides (INS 472e)
- Tartaric, acetic and fatty acid esters of mono-and diglyceride Tartaric (INS 472f)
- Lactic acid esters of mono- and diglycerides (INS 472b)
- Acetic acid esters of mono- and diglycerides (INS 472a)
- Momostarch phosphate (INS 1410)
- Riboflavin (INS 101i)
- Lecithin (INS 322)
- Lactitol (INS 966)
- Lysozyme hydrochloride (INS 1105)
- Processed euchema seaweed (INS 407 a)
- Starch sodium octenylsuccinate (INS 1450)
- Starch acetate (INS 1420)

- Stearyl citrate (INS 484)
- Stannous chloride (INS 512)
- Beetroot red (INS 162)Octyl gallate (INS 311)
- Aluminium silicate (INS 559)
- Aluminium stearate (INS 470)
- Aluminium ammonium sulfate (INS 523)
- Alpha-tocopherol (INS 307c)
- Agar (INS 406)
- Acacia (INS 414)
- Ethyl cellulose (INS 462)
- Ethyl paraben (INS 214)
- Ethyl ester of beta-apo-8'-carotenoic acid (INS 160f)
- Ethyl maltol (INS 637)
- Ethyl hydroxyethyl cellulose (INS 467)
- Erythrosine (INS 127)
- Erythritol (INS 968)
- Azodicarbonamide (INS 927a)
- Glocose oxidase (INS 1102)
- Enzyme treated starch (INS 1405)
- Blomelium (INS 1101 iii)
- Papain (INS 1101 ii)
- Alpha-amylase enzyme, Glycogenase (INS 1100)
- Protease from aspergillus oryzae, var. (INS 1100i)
- Lipase from aspergillus oryzae, var. (INS 1104)
- Acid treated starch (INS 1401)
- Ammonium glutamate (INS 624)
- Ammonium carbonate (INS 503i)
- Ammonium chloride (INS 510)
- Ammonium citrate (INS 380)
- Ammonium bicarbonate (INS 503ii)
- Ammonium lactate (INS 328)
- Ammonium acetate (INS 264)
- Ammonium alginate (INS 403)
- Ammonium hydroxide (INS 527)
- Ascorbyl palminate (INS 304)
- Ascorbyl stearate (INS 305)
- Alkali treated starch (INS 1402)
- Indigocarmine (INS 132)
- Acetylated distarch glycerol (INS 1423)
- Acetylated distarch phosphate (INS 1414)
- Acetylated distarch adipate (INS 1422)
- Acid treated starch (INS 1401)
- Oxidized starch (INS 1404)
- Oxystearin (INS 387)

- Ortho-phenyl phenol (INS 231)
- Isopropyl citrate mixture (INS 384)
- Isomalt (INS 953)
- Hexa methylene tetramine (INS 239)
- Hydroxypropyl cellulose (INS 463)
- Hydroxypropyl distarch phosphate (INS 1442)
- Hydroxypropyl methyl cellulose (INS 464)
- Hydroxypropyl starch (INS 1440)
- Ice structuring protein type III HPLC 12*

Section V. Pesticides and Other Contaminants:

Food containing pesticide residues and contaminants are enforced by the Ministry of Public Health's Food and Drug Administration (FDA). FDA establishes regulations and imposes maximum residue limits (MRLs) based on the MRL standards established by the National Bureau of Agricultural Commodity & Food Standards (NBACFS). In addition, the Department of Agriculture (DOA) in the Ministry of Agriculture and Cooperatives (MOAC) control the use of agricultural chemicals.

5.1 Food Containing Pesticide Residues

The tolerance levels for residues allowed in foodstuffs are defined as Extraneous Residue Limits (ERL) and Maximum Residue Limits (MRL). However, zero tolerance level is set for toxic substances in agriculture which are officially prohibited under the Notification of Ministry of Agriculture and Cooperatives, except for the established Extraneous Maximum Residue Limit. Under the Hazardous Substance Act (No. 3) B.E. 2551 (2008), the following substances are classified as Type 4 hazardous substances, which are prohibited for production, import, export, and possession:
- aldrin
- aminocarb
- aminodiphenyl
- amitrole
- aramite
- asbestos - amosite
- azinphos – ethyl
- azinphos - methyl
- benzidine
- beta - HCH 1,3,5/2,4,6 - hexachloro- cyclohexane
- BHC or HCH (1,2,3,4,5,6 - hexachloro-cyclohexane)
- binapacryl
- bis chloromethyl ether
- bromophos
- bromophos-ethyl
- cadmium and cadmium compounds
- calcium arsenate
- captafol
- carbon tetrachloride

- chlordane
- chlordecone
- chlordimeform
- chlorobenzilate
- chlorophenols
- chlorthiophos
- copper arsenate hydroxide
- cycloheximide
- cyhexatin
- daminozide
- DBCP (1,2-dibromo-3-chloropropane)
- DDT (1,1,1-trichloro-2,2-bis (4-chlorophenyl ethane))
- demephion
- demeton
- o-dichlorobenzene
- dieldrin
- dimefox
- dinoseb
- dinoterb
- disulfoton
- DNOC (4,6-dinitro-o-cresol)
- EDB (1,2-dibromoethane)
- endrin
- ethyl hexyleneglycol (ethyl hexane diool)
- ethylene dichloride
- ethylene oxide (1,2-epoxyethane)
- fensulfothion
- fentin
- fluoroacetamide
- fluoroacetate sodium
- fonofos
- heptachlor
- hexachlorobenzene
- lead arsenate
- leptophos
- lindane (>99% gamma-HCH gamma- BHC)
- MCPB [4-(4-chhloro-o-tolyloxy) butyric acid]
- mecoprop
- mephosfolan
- mercury compounds
- mevinphos
- MGK repellent - 11
- mirex
- monocrotophos

- napthylamine
- 4-nitrodiphenyl
- nitrofen
- parathion
- Paris green
- pentachlorophenate sodium pentachlorophenoxide sodium
- pentachlorophenol
- phenothiol
- phorate
- phosphamidon
- phosphorus
- polybrominated biphenyls, PBBs
- polychlorinated triphenyls, PCTs
- prothoate
- pyrinuron (piriminil)
- safrole
- schradan
- sodium arsenite
- sodium chlorate
- strobane (polychloroterpenes)
- sulfotep
- 2,4,5-T ([2,4,5-trichlorophenoxyl] acetic acid)
- 2,4,5-TCP (2,4,5-trichlorophenol)
- TDE or DDD [1,1-dichloro-2,2-bis (4-chlorophenyl) ethanel]
- TEPP (tetraethyl pyrophosphate)
- 2,4,5-TP ((+)-2-[2,4,5-trichlorophenoxy] propionic acid)
- thallium sulfate
- toxaphene or camphechlor
- tri (2,3-dibromopropyl) phosphate
- vinyl chloridemonomer (monochloroethene)
- methamidophos
- parathion methyl
- endosulfan

Codex-established pesticide MRLs are generally accepted. Detailed information on food containing pesticide residues is available in the Ministry of Public Health's Notification Re: Food Containing Pesticide Residues dated April 14, 2011 (See GAIN report TH9141).

5.2 Food Containing Contaminants

According to Ministerial Notification No. 98 of B.E. 2529 (1986) and Ministerial Notification No. 273 of B.E. 2546 (2003), food shall not contain contaminants with more than the following specifications.

1. Metal		
Tin	250	mg/kg
Zinc	100	mg/kg
Copper	20	mg/kg
Lead	1	mg/kg with the exception for foods that contain high amount of natural lead. Such foods shall seek the approval from FDA.
Inorganic Arsenic	2	mg/kg for fish and seafood
Total Arsenic	2	mg/kg for other foods
Mercury	0.5	mg/kg for seafood and not more than 0.02 mg/kg for other foods
2. Aflatoxin	20	mg/kg
3. Other contaminants shall be subjected to FDA approval.		

Note that the above regulations are not applicable to specifically-controlled food or other standardized food declared by the Ministry of Public Health and for which the quantity of contaminants may be specified otherwise by the Ministry.

The Thai FDA requires that all food products must be free of the following chemicals and their metabolites as stipulated in Ministry of Public Health's Notification No. 299 B.E. 2549 (2006) Re: Prescribed Standards for Some Chemical Contaminations in Foods (2nd Edition). A list of chemicals under this regulation include the following:

- Chloramphenicol and its salts
- Nitrofurazone and its salts
- Nitrofurantoin and its salts
- Furazolidone and its salts
- Furaltadone and its salts
- Malachite green and its salts

In addition, all food products must be free of β-Agonist chemical groups and its salts, including substances which are derived from its metabolites as stipulated in Ministry of Public Health's Notification No. 269 B.E. 2546 (2003) Re: Prescribed Standards for β-Agonist Chemicals Group Contamination in Foods.

An additional list of veterinary drugs covered by the regulation and a set of MRLs by animal species and organ tissue/product are available in Ministerial Notification No. 303 BE. 2550 (2007). Details of the new proposed rules are discussed in GAIN report TH7060.

5.3 Food Pathogens Control Measures in Food Products

Importers of 38 types of products listed under the Ministry of Public Health's Notification No. 364 Re: Food Standards as Regards Pathogens B.E. 2556 (2013) must present a lab analysis report during the food product registration process to ensure that imported products are pathogen free or their presence does not exceed maximum specified limits stated in the notification. The Thai FDA accepts lab analyses reports issued by government laboratories from the country of origin, government laboratories in Thailand, private laboratories accredited by the Thai government or laboratories accredited by international accreditation agencies.

5.4 Yeast and Mold Level in Foods

In September 2010, the Thai FDA revised and set new tolerance level for yeast and mold in six food categories: beverages in sealed containers, coffee, tea, chocolate, weight control foods, and electrolyte. The background of the notification and the established tolerance levels for yeast and mold in foods are available under GAIN report TH0144.

Section VI. Other Regulations and Requirements:
6.1 Laboratory Testing

To register specifically-controlled foods with the Thai FDA, the Lab Analysis Report is required to: ensure that the products meet standard requirements under product related ministerial notifications, be free from microbial organisms and toxic chemical substances that are not safe for consumption, and ensure that products are of good nutritional quality. The Thai FDA accepts a Lab Analysis Report for required food product issued by government laboratory from the country of origin, government laboratory in Thailand or the private laboratory accredited by Thai government. The submitted lab analysis report should not be older than one year. The analysis results must comply with the quality or standard specified in the Ministerial notification. More information on a Lab Analysis Report is available in GAIN report TH8116.

6.2 Shelf Life and Packaging

Shelf longevity and packaging are critical issues. The long shipping time and the likelihood that products will pass through multiple marketing channels before reaching consumers should be considered. Due to Thailand's hot and humid climate, moisture resistant outer and inner packaging should be used to preserve product quality.

6.3 Product Samples and Mail Order Shipments

A limited amount of processed or packaged food samples for product registration and consideration for purchase can be brought in without an import license from the FDA. However, samples of raw, fresh or frozen foodstuffs (e.g. meat, vegetables and fruits) may be subject to other regulations established by the concerned authorities. In certain cases, a health certificate, sanitary certificate, or phytosanitary certificate will be required. Mail order shipments of products for sale are also subject to the same rules and regulations imposed by the FDA and other relevant authorities as those of regular imports. For more information, see details in the following sections.

6.4 Import Control Under the Tariff Rate Quota (TRQ)

Thailand is permitted to establish TRQs for 23 agricultural products under the WTO Agreement on Agriculture. The products under the TRQs system are divided into two groups. The first group comprises a number of traditional export commodities (e.g. rice, coconuts), where comparative advantage could preclude the need for import protection. A second group consists of commodities, which can be produced domestically, but importation is necessary to meet the high demand of the processing industry (e.g. oilseed, corn). In administering the TRQs for the latter group, the Royal Thai Government (RTG) will issue higher-than commitment in-quota amounts and/or lower-than-commitment in-quota duties when domestic production is not sufficient to cover the demand, especially for export-oriented industries. In years of sufficient domestic supply or surpluses, the RTG will limit in quota imports, both in-quota amount and in-quota duties, only to the level which is obligated under the WTO agreement. More details on the tariff-rate quotas and the out-of quota tariff rates are provided in FAS/Bangkok's Trade Policy Monitoring Annual Report 2013.
The covered commodities under the TRQ system are listed as follows:

- Milk and cream, and flavored milk
- Skim milk
- Potato
- Onion
- Garlic
- Coconut
- Copra
- Coffee bean
- Tea
- Pepper (piper nigrum L.)
- Corn
- Rice
- Soybeans
- Onion seeds
- Soybean oil
- Palm and palm oil
- Coconut oil
- Sugar
- Instant coffee
- Soybean meal
- Tobacco leaf
- Raw silk
- Dried longan

The Department of Foreign Trade, Ministry of Commerce monitors imports of these products and requires that any importer must apply for an import permit.

6.5 Specific Import Control on Animals and Animal Products

Through the Animal Epidemics Act B.E. 2499 (1956), the Department of Livestock Development (DLD) of the Ministry of Agriculture and Cooperatives directly monitors the importation of meat. An import permit from DLD is required for these products, frozen or chilled. Prior to importation, an application for a permit should be completed and submitted to the Animal Quarantine Station at the port (sea or air) of entry where the products will be shipped, whether by air or by sea. Also, a health certificate is needed. Upon entry, the Animal Quarantine Station must inspect the products prior to release by the Thai Customs. Generally, a U.S. health certificate is acceptable. However, the DLD may re-inspect imported meat and livestock on a random basis as they enter Thailand.

The DLD also collects import permit fees on uncooked red meat, poultry, and meat offal, mainly to protect domestic producers. Fees on red meat (beef, buffalo meat, goat meat, lamb, and pork) are 5 baht/kg (US$ 156/ton), followed by 10 baht/kg (US$ 313/ton) for poultry meat and 5 baht/kg (US$ 156/ton) for offal.

6.6 Specific Import Control on Beef and Beef Products from BSE-Affected Countries

The Ministry of Public Health (MOPH) also officially notified on January 13, 2005 the lifting of its ban on imports and sales of certain bovine products from BSE-risk countries, including the United States. The products covered in this notification include:

- Milk and milk products;
- Hides and skins;
- Gelatin and collagen prepared from hides and skins;
- Gelatin and collagen prepared from bone;
- Protein-free tallow (maximum level of insoluble impurities of 0.15% in weight) and derivatives made from this tallow;
- Dicalcium phosphate (with no trace of protein or fat);
- Deboned skeletal muscle meat and its products from cattle 30 months of age or less, which were not subject to a stunning process, prior to slaughter, with a device injecting compressed air or gas into the cranial cavity, or to a pithing process, and which were subject to ante-mortem and post-mortem inspections and were not suspect or confirmed BSE cases, and which has been prepared in a manner to avoid contamination with tissues listed in Article 2.3.13.13 of OIE Terrestrial Animal Health Code 2005. BSE-risk tissues are brains, tonsil glands, spinal cords, eyes, etc.;
- Blood and blood by-products, from cattle which were not subject to a stunning process, prior to slaughter, with a device injecting compressed air or gas into the cranial cavity or to a pithing process.

Thailand restricts imports of U.S. bone-in-beef and related products due to the detection of a BSE positive animal in the United States in 2003. Currently, Thailand only allows import of U.S. deboned beef from animals less than 30 months of age. In order to import uncooked boneless beef, exporters must meet the following MOAC/DLD import protocol requirements.

1) A health certificate in English signed by a full-time authorized veterinary official of the U.S. Department of Agriculture's (USDA) Food Safety Inspection Service (FSIS) stating:

1.1 Type of cuts and package of the meat/meat products.

1.2 Number of pieces or package and net weight.

1.3 Names and addresses and registered number of the approved manufacturers.

1.4 Names and addresses of the exporter and the consignee.

1.5 Dates of slaughter, manufacture or packaging and export.

1.6 Certification of condition items (2) to (10).

2) The United States is free from rinder pest and foot-and-mouth disease (FMD) and officially approved by the Office International des Epizooties (OIE) for at least 3 (three) years prior to export.

3) The farm(s) or premises of origin have been free from contagious bovine pleuropneumonia during the past 12 (twelve) months preceding the slaughter of the animals and until the time of export. The animals received ante and post mortem inspection and were found healthy and free of clinical signs of the following diseases: tuberculosis, toxoplasmosis, taeniasis, and bovine cysticercosis.

4) The product was obtained from animals of U.S. origin or legally imported in accordance with U.S. import requirements.

5) The cattle have received ante-mortem and post-mortem inspections by FSIS veterinarian or may be performed by an official FSIS inspector with appropriate training, knowledge, skills and abilities.

6) The product was obtained from animals less than thirty (30) months of age. The product was obtained from animals which were not stunned by means of gas injection in the cranial cavity or cutting of the spinal cord by laceration of the central nervous tissue by means of introducing a sharp cutting instrument in the cranial cavity or by a pithing process. The product contains no specified risk materials including brain, skull, eyes, trigeminal ganglia, spinal cord, tonsils, distal ileum, vertebral column (excluding the vertebrae of the tail, the transverse processes of the thoracic and lumbar vertebrae, and the wings of the sacrum), and dorsal root ganglia. The product does not contain meat from advanced meat recovery and mechanically separated meat. The meat was derived from animals which received ante and post mortem inspection. The meat was not derived from animals that were known suspect or confirmed BSE cases.

7) The slaughter, processing, and storage of the product were from establishment(s) under federal inspection.

8) The meat contains no preservatives, additives or other substances posing a harmful risk to human health.

9) The meat has been produced according to a residue and microbiological sampling program in accordance with the USDA regulatory requirements.

10) The meat was produced in accordance with the FSIS National Residue Program.

11) The vehicles and containers used for transporting the exported boneless beef should be thoroughly cleaned and disinfected immediately prior to export.

12) The wrapping and packaging materials of the boneless beef portions must bear a health mark or inspection legend of the USDA. All shipping cartons of the boneless beef must bear slaughter or production date (month, day and year) on the cartons at the time of shipping and must be marked "Product of USA." The health mark label must be applied on the carton and the carton will be closed in a manner whereby tampering would be evident.

13) The boneless beef shall be subjected to inspection/detention for laboratory testing up on arrival in Thailand. The owner/importer shall be fully charged for incurred expenses.

14) Failure to follow the import procedures may result in returning the meat/meat products to the

country of origin or destroying without compensation.

In 2012, Thailand published new rules that largely align its BSE-related requirements with OIE guidelines. In August 2013, a team from the Thai Department of Livestock and Development conducted an audit of the U.S. beef production system as a step towards reopening the market to all U.S. beef products. Final approval for restoring full market access is pending agreement on an import protocol. Separately, the Thai Food and Drug Administration (FDA) has also claimed jurisdiction over the import of the same products based on food safety standards. USDA has been working with the Thai FDA to ensure its regulations comply with the OIE guidelines on BSE. The FDA rule revision, however, has been stalled following political turmoil and a military coup in Thailand. The new FDA rule is expected to be finalized in the first half to 2015 with the appointment of a new government.

6.7 Specific Import Control on Pork Meat

In 2012, Thailand indicated it would lift its ban on imports of pork from countries that allow the use of ractopamine after the Codex established Maximum Residue Levels (MRLs) for ractopamine in cattle and pig tissues. Since that time, Thailand has undertaken a two-year risk assessment of ractopamine, which is not expected to be finalized until 2015. As a result Thailand has not yet established MRLs for ractopamine in pork, which effectively prevents import of U.S. product. Separately, reports continue to indicate that there is use of ractopamine throughout the Thai pork industry and that Thai butchers request pork carcasses from animals treated with ractopamine because they producer higher yields.

6.8 Specific Import Control on Seafood

Imports of seafood, frozen or chilled, are under the supervision of Thai FDA. Basically, an import permit (normally granted shipment by shipment) is needed, together with a permit for distribution.

6.9 Specific Import Control on Fruits and Vegetables

Thailand's Plant Quarantine Act (No. 3) B.E. 2551 came into effect on August 28, 2008. The Act combined previous Ministerial Notifications from 2007 requiring Pest Risk Assessments (PRA) for imported plant materials as well as established broader powers for the Plant Quarantine Committee. The details of the Act can be viewed in GAIN report TH8047. On September 12, 2008, the Director General of the Department of Agriculture (DOA) officially notified guidelines for the importation of prohibited, restricted and non-prohibited articles (See GAIN report TH8161).

The table below highlights import requirements under the current Plant Quarantine Act:

	PRA Approval	Import Permit	PC	Specific condition
Prohibited Articles:				
• imported for experiment and research		X	X	Limit point of Entry (POC)
• imported for commercial	X	X	X	No limit POC
• imported for other purpose	X	X	X	No limit POC
• transit to the 3rd country	X	X	X	No limit POC
Restricted Articles (import or transit)			X	No limit POC
Non-Prohibited Articles (import or transit)			X	No limit POC

Under an agreement between USDA and the Thai DOA Pest Risk Assessments (PRA) requirements for the following U.S. products have been temporarily waived (articles): 1) apple, 2) apricot, 3) cherry, 4) currant, 5) fig, 6) grape, 7) nectarine, 8) peach, 9) pear, 10) plum, 11) prune, 12) strawberry, 13) seed potato, 14) table potato, 15) sorghum grain, 16) sorghum seed, 17) sweet pepper, 18) corn seed, and 19) eggplant.

In 2009, the DOA completed the PRA process for U.S. potatoes, including seed potatoes, potatoes for processing and potatoes for consumption. To date, the DOA has not initiated PRAs for other U.S. plant products besides potatoes. Due to the waivers, U.S. products on the above list other than seed and table potatoes are currently allowed to be traded under import requirements established before implementation of the 2008 Plant Quarantine Act. These import requirements will remain in effect until the PRAs for these products are completed and the new import protocols are endorsed.

Import Requirements for Seed Potatoes

The importer of seed potatoes must work with the Ministry of Commerce's Department of Foreign Trade (DFT/MOC), the Ministry of Agriculture and Cooperatives' Department of Agriculture (DOA /MOAC), and the Ministry of Commerce's Customs Department.

DFT/MOC administers the tariff-rate-quota system for seed potatoes. The DFT sets the TRQ each year and notifies its allocation of seed potato import quota to companies and cooperatives. These companies are normally potato chip processors in Thailand which contract fresh potato production with small farmers in the northern provinces. Eligible importers receive a certain amount of import quota which is subject to an in-quota tariff rate of 27 percent. Otherwise, out-of-quota imports are subject to 125 percent tariff rate. Once the quota is allocated, the importers need to register with DFT, which will provide specific documentation on the import terms. The importer must then present this documentation to Thai Customs for clearance and the application of the corresponding fees. On March 27, 2012, the Ministry of Commerce announced its 2012-2014 plans for administering its quota allocation for seed potatoes and potatoes for processing. Under the plan, the quota for seed potatoes in a given year can be unlimited and there is no specific import window period.

Under DOA/MOAC's current import process, U.S. seed potatoes must abide by following protocol: 1) Be produced in California, Idaho, Oregon, and Washington; 2) Importers must apply for a phytosanitary import permit with the DOA prior to import; and 3) Shipments of seed potatoes must be accompanied by a phytosanitary certificate (PC) that contains the following statement: *"The seed potatoes in this consignment were produced in the United States of America in accordance with the conditions governing entry of seed potatoes to Thailand."*

Import Requirements for Potatoes for Processing

Like seed potatoes, the importer of potatoes for processing must work with Ministry of Commerce's Department of Foreign Trade (DFT/MOC), DOA /MOAC, and the Ministry of Commerce's Customs Department.

DFT/MOC administers the tariff-rate-quota system for potatoes for processing. Each year, the DFT notifies its allocation of import quota on potato for processing to chip processing companies in Thailand. Eligible companies are allocated import quotas which are subject to an in-quota tariff rate of 27 percent. Otherwise, out-of-quota imports are subject to 125 percent tariff rate. Like seed potatoes, the importer needs to contact the DFT to register and receive specific documentation regarding the terms of the importation. The importer has to present this documentation to Thai Customs for clearance and pay the corresponding fees. On March 27, 2012, the Ministry of Commerce announced its 2012-2014 plans for administering quota allocations for seed potatoes and potatoes for processing. Under the plan, the quota for potatoes used for processing in a given year is limited to no more than 36,000 metric tons and import window period is limited to July-December for each year.

Under DOA/MOAC's current import protocol, potatoes from all states are allowed except where potato cyst nematode is regulated and/or soil that is contaminated with the nematode. Currently, importers are limited to potato chip processors in Thailand that comply with DOA's guidelines on the safe disposal of soil, culls, and water. The importer must apply for a phytosanitary import permit with the DOA prior to an import. The product shipment must be accompanied by a phytosanitary certificate (PC) that contains the following statements: *"The potatoes in this consignment were produced in the United States of America in accordance with the conditions governing entry of potatoes for processing to Thailand and inspected and found to be free of quarantine pests."* And *"The potatoes in this consignment have been washed"* or *"The potatoes in this consignment were treated with a sprout inhibitor."*

Import Requirements for Potatoes for Consumption (Table-Stock Potatoes)

The importer of potatoes for consumption must work with MOC/MOC, MOAC/DOA, FDA, and MOF/Customs Department.

Unlike seed potatoes and potatoes for processing, DFT/MOC does not apply a tariff-rate-quota system for table-stock potatoes. As a result, all imports of table-stock potatoes are considered as out-of-quota imports which are subject to 125 percent tariff rate. To import potatoes, the importer needs to contact the DFT to register and receive documentation specifying the terms of the import. The importer must then present the documents to Customs Department for clearance and for the application of the corresponding fees.

Like potatoes for processing, DOA/MOAC allows imports from all U.S. states except the production area where potato cyst nematode is regulated and/or presents in the soil. There is no specific requirement that the importer must be a chip processor. As in the previous cases, the importer must apply for a phytosanitary import permit with the DOA prior to an import. The product shipment must be accompanied by a phytosanitary certificate (PC) that contains the following statements: *"The potatoes in this consignment were produced in the United States of America in accordance with the conditions governing entry of potatoes for consumption to Thailand and inspected and found to be free of quarantine pests."* and *"The potatoes in this consignment have been washed."*

In addition, table-stock potatoes are considered a food item under the current Food Act of 1979; as such, importers must apply for and receive a food import permit prior to importation from the FDA. Prior to granting a permit, the FDA will inspect the importer's storage facilities for compliance. When a shipment is cleared, the importer must present the food import permit to FDA and Customs inspectors at the port. If all is in order, the shipment will be cleared for release. In case a substance is found that is either on the pesticide ban list or above established MRL's, the shipment must be returned or destroyed.

Section VII. Other Specific Standards:

Each food product listed in the food category table in Section I has its specific product standards/requirements. The FDA is the regulating authority. Special labeling regulations on some products are provided below. Detailed information on particular products can be obtained from the Food Control Division, FDA.

7.1 Quality Labeling

In general, wordings or statements that imply or mark product quality such as "premium grade" or "grade A" are considered misleading by the FDA, thus are prohibited.

7.2 Alcoholic Beverages

Labeling requirements for alcoholic beverages are stipulated in Ministerial Notification No. 275 of B.E. 2540 (1997).

On February 13, 2008, the Alcohol Consumption Control Act was published in the Royal Gazette. The Act is intended to curb alcohol consumption through several measures including health warning labeling, restriction on selling places of alcohol beverage, limiting selling period, limiting selling alcohol beverage to persons under 20 years old, prohibiting sales by vending machine, prohibiting price discount and some types of sale promotions, prohibiting direct advertisement that encourages increased consumption. Additional details on this Act are available in GAIN report TH8030.

7.3 Coffee Drink

Labeling requirements for coffee drinks are stipulated in Ministerial Notification No. 276 of B.E. 2540 (1997).

7.4 Tea Drink

Labeling requirements for tea drinks are stipulated in Ministerial Notification No. 277 of B.E. 2540 (1997).

Section VIII. Copyright and/or Trademark Laws:

A patent application shall be filed with the Department of Intellectual Property. An applicant domiciled abroad must be represented by one of the patent agents registered with the Department of Intellectual Property.

Protecting industrial rights is basically the responsibility of each company. A foreign patent which has not been granted a separate patent in Thailand receives no protection under the Patent Act. However, foreign patent holders in foreign countries may enter into business transactions with parties in Thailand and seek equivalent protection through contractual obligations in the form of a licensing agreement. Note that this protection can be enforced only between contractual parties, it will not create any rights to take action against a third party.

Since foreign patents receive no protection under the Thailand's Patent Act, no civil or criminal action can be taken against a third party who produces or sells a patented product in Thailand.

International copyrights are well defined in the Copyright Act of B.E. 2537 (1994). A copyrighted work of a creator and rights of a performer whose country is a party to the Treaty for the Protection of Copyrights or the Treaty for the Performer's Rights to which Thailand is a party, or a copyrighted work of an international organization of which Thailand is a member shall be protected by the Act.

The Trademark Act of B.E. 2534 (1991), as amended by the Trademark Act (No 2) B.E. 2543 (2000), governs registration and provides protection for trademarks. Included in the Act is a prohibition on importing objects bearing marks which are similar to or counterfeit of trademarks registered with the Trademark Office.

Well-known marks are protected in Thailand by two methods. The first one is preventative in nature as it is embodied in the registration process. The trademark registrar will refuse to register any mark which is identical or similar to the well-known mark, misleading or confusing the public as to the proprietor or origin of the goods. The second one is correction in nature. In the case that the mark has already been registered, any interested party or the registrar may file a petition to the Trademark Board to order the revocation of such mark if it can be proved that the mark is not registerable under the Trademark Act.

Nonetheless, it is basically the responsibility of each proprietor to have a separate trademark registration in Thailand. A trademark applicant must be completed by the proprietor or his appointed attorney/agent in Thai and filed with the Department of Intellectual Property on official forms. The proprietor or his attorney or agent must have a place of business or address in Thailand which the Department can contact.

Section IX. Import Procedures:

Imported goods may not legally enter into Thailand until the shipment has arrived at specified port of entry and delivery of the merchandise has been authorized by the Thai Customs Department. This is normally accomplished by filing the appropriate documents, either by the importer or by its agent.

The Customs Department does not notify the importer of the arrival of a shipment. Notification is usually made by the carrier of the goods. The importer should make their own arrangements to be sure that they or their agent will be informed of the arrival of shipment immediately so that the entry can be filed and delays in obtaining the goods are avoided.

9.1 Custom Duties

Imports arriving by air, sea or land have a clearance process which is similar to that carried out in most other countries. In order to clear goods arriving by sea, the importer has to go to the Customs House and file an entry form, together with all relevant documents, such as the invoice, packing list, a copy of bill of lading, and import declaration. Import documents, if translated into Thai, will help expedite customs clearance. In cases where imports are subject to business tax, the importer is also required to have a business tax registration number.

After these documents have been processed and the goods have arrived, the importer must pay applicable tariff duties and business taxes. In cases where total duties have not been determined or where urgent clearance is necessary, a deposit may be made. The documents must be taken to the warehouse and presented to an inspector who will make a report on the entry form. If there is a discrepancy, the goods will be retained until additional duty or a fine is paid. The Port Authority will then calculate landing and storage charges based upon the size or gross weight of the package. After paying these charges, the importer must submit receipts and the release order or delivery order to obtain a warehouse receipt which will allow the imported goods to be claimed. With proper documents, the entire customs clearance normally takes 2-3 days.

For disputed and/or rejected products, an appeal can be made with the Legal Affairs Bureau, Customs Department.

9.2 Customs Clearance of Prepacked Foodstuffs

Prepackaged foodstuffs will need additional inspection by related authorities before proceeding to regular customs formalities. In addition to the FDA, other concerned officers such as animal quarantine officers, plant quarantine officers, and fisheries department officers are stationed at the port of entry to determine whether certain imported foodstuffs meet the requirements set by their agencies. In such cases, certain certificates (i.e. health certificate or phytosanitary certificate) may be required. More detailed information is contained in the relevant sections of this report.

Appendix I. Government Regulatory Agency Contacts:

FOOD AND DRUG ADMINISTRATION, MINISTRY OF PUBLIC HEALTH

Food Bureau
Tivanont Road, Muang
Nonthaburi 11000
Tel: (662) 590-7178
Fax: (662) 591-8460
E-mail: food@fda.moph.go.th

Inspection Division
Tivanont Road, Muang
Nonthaburi 11000
Tel: (662) 590-7323
Fax: (662) 591-8477
E-mail: inspection@fda.moph.go.th

DEPARTMENT OF MEDICAL SCIENCES, MINISTRY OF PUBLIC HEALTH
Food Analysis Division
Department of Medical Sciences
Soi Bumratnaradul Hospital
Muang, Nonthaburi 11000
Tel: (662) 951-0000 Ext. 99967
Fax: (662) 951-1023

DEPARTMENT OF FOREIGN TRADE, MINISTRY OF COMMERCE
Bureau of Trade Measures
Department of Foreign Trade
Sanam Bin Nam-Nonthaburi Road
Nonthaburi 11000
Tel: (662) 547-4737
Fax: (662) 547-4736
E-mail: cdtdft@moc.go.th

Bureau of National Imports-Exports Product Standards
Department of Foreign Trade
Sanam Bin Nam-Nonthaburi Road
Nonthaburi 11000
Tel: (662) 547-4746
Fax: (662) 547-4816
E-mail: tpdft@moc.go.th

DEPARTMENT OF LIVESTOCK, MINISTRY OF AGRICULTURE AND COOPERATIVES
Animal Quarantine Inspection Services
Department of Livestock Development

Phyathai Road
Bangkok 10400
Tel: (662) 653-4444 Ext. 4110
Fax: (662) 653-4865
E-mail: dcontrol8@dld.go.th

Bangkok Seaport Animal Quarantine Station
Klong Toey Port
Klongtoey
Bangkok 10110
Tel: (662) 249-2112
Fax: (662) 249-4358

Suvarnabhumi Airport Animal Quarantine Station
Samut Prakarn 10540
Tel: (662) 134-0731
Fax: (662) 134-3640

DEPARTMENT OF FISHERIES, MINISTRY OF AGRICULTURE AND COOPERATIVES
Fisheries Resources Conservation Division
Contact: Chief of Fisheries Administration & Management Section, Department of Fisheries
Kasetsart University, Chatuchak
Bangkok 10900
Tel: (662) 562-0600/15, ext 3509
Fax: (662) 562-0528
E-mail: fishtradeins@dof.thaigov.net

DEPARTMENT OF AGRICULTURE, MINISTRY OF AGRICULTURE AND COOPERATIVES
Plant Quarantine Subdivision
Office of Agricultural Regulation
Department of Agriculture
Chatuchak, Bangkok 10900
Tel: (662) 940-6573, 940-6670 Ext. 102
Fax : (662) 579-4129

Plant Quarantine Station
Suvarnabhumi Airport
Samut Prakarn 10540
Tel: (662) 134-0717

EXCISE DEPARTMENT, MINISTRY OF FINANCE
Department of Intellectual Property
44/100 Nonthaburi 1 Rd.
Bangkrasor, Muang

Nonthaburi 11000
Tel: (662) 547-4685-6
Fax: (662) 547-4681

DEPARTMENT OF INTELLECTUAL PROPERTY, MINISTRY OF COMMERCE
License Subdivision
Bureau of Tax Administration 1
Excise Department
1488 Nakhon Chaisri Road
Bangkok 10300
Tel/Fax: (662) 243-0525

CUSTOMS DEPARTMENT, MINISTRY OF FINANCE
Import Formalities Division
Customs Department
Klong Toey, Bangkok 10110
Tel: (662) 249-4266, 671-5250
Fax: (662) 249-4297
Legal Affairs Bureau
Customs Department
Klong Toey, Bangkok 10110
Tel: (662) 671-7560, ext. 9310, 9311
Fax: (662) 671-7626

Appendix II. Other Import Specialist Contacts:
U.S. EMBASSY
Foreign Agricultural Service
U.S. Embassy
120-122 Wireless Road
Bangkok 10330
Tel: (662) 205-5106
Fax: (662) 255-2907
E-mail: agbangkok@fas.usda.gov

CODEX CONTACT:
National Bureau of Agricultural Commodity and Food Standards
Office of Commodity and System Standard
50 Phaholyothin Rd.
Bangkok 10900
Tel: (662) 561-3390 ext 1101
Fax: (662) 561-3697
E-mail: acfs@acfs.go.th

AMERICAN CHAMBER OF COMMERCE
GPF Building, Tower A, 7th Floor

93/1 Wireless Road
Bangkok 10330
Tel: 662-254-1041-5
Fax: 662-251-1605
E-mail: info@amchamthailand.com

U.S. DAIRY EXPORT COUNCIL
Southeast Asian Representative Office
U.S. Dairy Export Council
P.O. Box 1492
Nana Post Office
Bangkok 10110
Tel: (662) 689-6311
Fax: (662) 689-6314
E-mail: usdec@pacrimassociates.com

U.S. DRY PEA AND LENTIL COUNCIL
AgriSource Co.,Ltd.
No. 416, 4th Fl., Ambassador's Court
76/1 Soi Langsuan
Ploenchit Road
Bangkok 10330
Tel: (662) 251-8655/6, 251-8669, 251-8772
Fax: (662) 251-0390
E-mail: agsource@loxinfo.co.th

AMERICAN SOYBEAN ASSOCIATION
Thailand Representative
59/43 Baan Klangmuang
Ladprao 71 Road
Bangkok 10230
Tel. (662) 539-5373, 539-5332
Fax (662) 539-5256
E-mail: asathai@loxinfo.co.th

UNITED STATES POTATO BOARD
Thailand Representative
2 Soi Farm Wattana,
Phrakanong, Klongtoey,
Bangkok 10110
Tel: (6681) 753-1000
Fax: (662) 381-1437
Email: kraipob@pangsapa.com

NORTHWEST CHERRY BOARD
Thailand, Singapore and Malaysia Representative
PT&Tatch Ltd.
208 Soi Ram-Indra 19
Ram-Indra Road, Anusa-waree,
Bangkhen, Bangkok 10220
Tel: (662) 521-2170/970/8207
Fax: (662) 970-8208
Email: pt@tatch.in.th

WASHINGTON APPLE COMMISSION
At Success Marketing Co., Ltd.
7th Floor, Room 7-01,
Ploenchit Center
2 Sukhumvit Road, Klongtoey
Bangkok 10110 Thailand
Contact: Ms. Apiradee (Tulip) Phanuroote, Manager
Tel: (662) 656-7921
Fax: (662) 656-7931
Email: tulip@successmarketing.co.th

CALIFORNIA MILK ADVISORY BOARD
At Success Marketing Co., Ltd.
7th Floor, Room 7-01,
Ploenchit Center
2 Sukhumvit Road, Klongtoey
Bangkok 10110 Thailand
Contact: Ms. Theeravee Ungkuvorakul, Managing Director
Tel: (662) 656-7921
Fax: (662) 656-7931
Email: theeravee@successmarketing.co.th